a little sweet,
a little sour

sera gandhi

illustrated by
priyanka pachpande

Disclaimer

SUPER FAST AUTHOR
www.superfastauthor.com

Registered Office- 604, Mayur Vatika, Dapodi Pune 411001
Website: https://www.superfastauthor.com
Email: superfastauthor@gmail.com

First Published by SUPERFASTAUTHOR 2020

Copyright © SERA GANDHI 2020

Title: A LITTLE SWEET, A LITTLE SOUR
Price: INR 199 / $ 6.99
All Rights Reserved.
ISBN 978-81-948673-2-6

LIMITS OF LIABILITY/DISCLAIMER OF WARRANTY

Dedicated to my loving
grandparents who inspire
me every day

Preface

"I have never started a poem whose end I knew.
Writing a poem is discovering"
~ Robert Frost

Poetry was and still is a medium of self-discovery for me. The emotions I couldn't express verbally, often ended up being the driving forces for my poetry. The poems in this book are simply those scrawled emotions that I felt through my early adolescent years.

Almost all of them are based on incidents that happened around me. 'With love, humanity' is particularly dear to me as I remember writing it in 30 minutes straight. I had just come home from a rainy school day and the news about the Elphinstone Bridge stampede in Mumbai had a very deep impact on me. I just poured my heart out and let my thoughts flow. It was the first time I discovered how liberating it was to write. 'Dark' is another poem that has a very special place in my heart. I had never spoken openly about my insecurity and my struggles with self-image, but after I finished this poem – I could feel the empowerment run through my veins. I finally felt like I had overcome my insecurity. Others like 'Hurt', 'Strength', and 'Move On' are also outcomes of personal experiences.

'Last Words' and 'Bahadur' are slightly different as I've experimented with fictional poetry in those. 'Treasure' tells another one of the stories that I imagined about a boy and his dying grandad. If it were up to me, I would probably say that 'A colourful monochrome' is my best attempt at poetry so far. It was the first time that I took an abstract idea from my brain and tried to create something with it.

Dieter F. Uchtdorf has wisely said, 'The desire to create is one of the deepest yearnings of the human soul.' Poetry helps me create and creating helps me move forward every day with a smile.

While this may not be the finest set of poems you'll come across, I hope that at least some of them resonate with you and maybe even leave you with warmth and happiness in your heart.

Contents

LastWords

18/05/17

Last Words

Underneath the afternoon sun,

Lay a girl covered in liquid crimson,

The resplendent rays didn't seem so anymore,

Her body felt numb, her limbs too sore;

She remembered the blade pushed in,

In – into her abdomen,

She remembered the wicked laugh,

 She remembered the pain,

All of a sudden – her own name,

Her family, her friends,

All flashed before her eyes,

Almost immediately,

Tears welled up in her eyes;

There was a loud siren and then she saw a man,

This was her chance,

She could hardly breathe but tried as she can,

She knew she had to speak,

Speak for the last time,

For she knew it was happening,

Knew she was dying;

Her heart slowed down, the world disappeared,

But she wanted to say something,

Something that would be remembered,

So she slowly opened her lips;

Her eyes fought hard,

As did her tongue,

Almost everything was gone, even her lung,

Using all of what was left in her body,

She tenuously said,

"Life is much prettier inside one's head."

With love, humanity

30/09/18

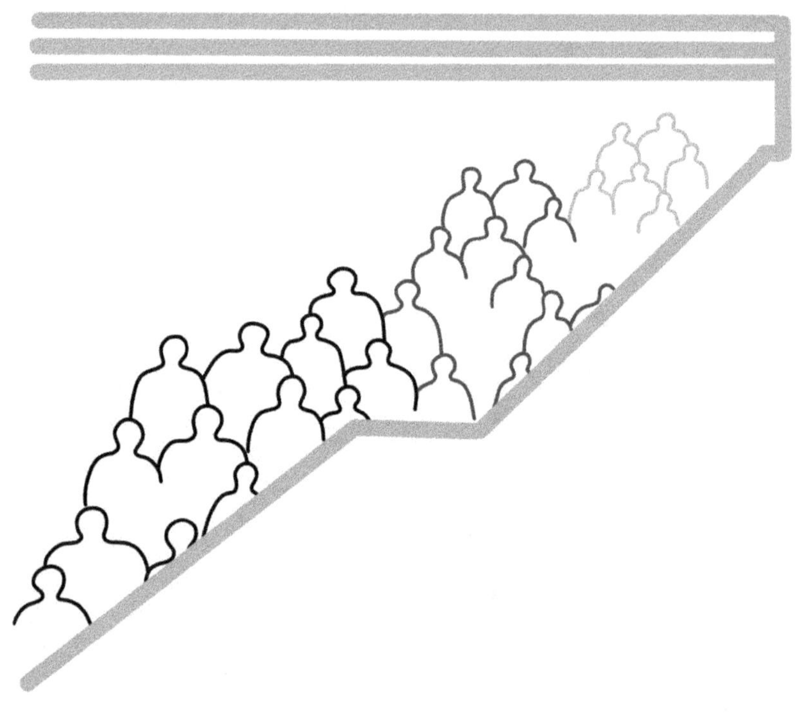

With love, humanity

Thundering sky,
Misty morning,
The wind blew wild,
Without any warning,

Mumbai had seen this weather,
Over and over again,
It was the "same old story,"
But what happened then,

A mammoth disaster,
Heart wrenching incident,
Elphinstone Bridge will never be the same,
Isn't it very, very evident?

The sky was crashing into the soil,
But those who have to toil,
Set out to earn their daily bread,
Just another rainy day they said,

They waited patiently,
Taking the bridge's shade,

It would stop eventually,
The rainy haze would fade,

Three local trains, coincidently together,
Reached the station,
And people flooded out,
Creating a commotion,

It was crowded and chaotic,
Just like any other day,
But what happened next,
Will shroud the sun's every ray,

A sharp noise and a part of the roof came down,
Someone yelled that the bridge was collapsing
Chaos ensued,
Everyone was running and gasping,

Where did their humanity go?
Why did the people trample each other?
Where was the civic sense?
Suddenly no one was a sister, none a brother,

Stampede is what they call it,

But simple stamping and crowd,

Doesn't make something a massacre,

It takes much, much more to make a shroud,

A mother of an 8- month old,

A 7 year old boy,

20 others gone,

Was their life just another ploy?

But in all of this mess,

People still talk about politics,

About bullet trains and leaders,

Forgetting the true antics,

Reality is,

That people have lost their humanity,

Lost their sense,

Sanity turned into insanity,

But insanity

Can't be the reason,

For the death of these people,

That would be treason,

So here I stand,

One girl, all alone,

Standing and pleading to the 1 billion Indians who live,

Let us learn to live- not as beasts, but as humans- let's payback that loan,

Our soldiers don't stand at the borders,

All mighty and strong,

Just to hear that their little son,

Was trampled, himself doing no wrong,

So let's payback that loan,

The one we owe our soldiers who boldly stand,

Those freedom fighters,

Let us give back to our country, our motherland,

Let us turn insanity back to sanity,

Let us remember the children, women and men,

Who died at Elphinstone,

Yes, let's be human again.

We Shall Overcome

15/11/2017

We Shall Overcome

We shall overcome,

A baseless, untrue line,

But to this falsehood we all succumb,

That eventually it'll be alright, it'll be fine,

We'll evolve, develop and improve~

Ourselves, we'll change with the times,

Remove injustice and prove~

That we are sensible enough, not to give in to these crimes,

Social evil,

Oh what a meagre term,

For the harsh, inhumane acts carried out on free will,

Yet with the criminals we aren't firm,

Raping minors as young as four,

Treating the women like toys,

Acid attacks and ill treatment galore,

But of course boys will be boys!

Corruption runs rampant,

Almost every day we bribe policemen,

The rich always declared "the innocent,"

How can we still believe in the next gen?

Yet we feel that someday,

Things will change,

So we bow our heads and pray,

To reach the other side of this escarped mountain range,

But what we urgently need,

Is not blind faith,

But courage and hard work indeed,

To actually do something and stop this hate,

We cannot rely,

On the hope of a better tomorrow,

No, we cannot sit and cry,

We have to step up and shun this sorrow,

So stop just hoping for a brighter future,

Instead start "working" towards it,

Raise your voices and create that first suture,

Because if you can imagine it, you can do it,

We are the ones who can weave,

Our future, ignore the rest,

So that when this world we leave,

We leave it in peace – knowing that we gave our best,

It doesn't matter who does what,

Doesn't matter what they think,

They're just a cowardly, misbelieving lot,

But we have to rise above and be the link,

The link that will be,

The end of this mad mess,

The first root of the new tree,

The tree of hope and happiness,

So let's begin by completing (entirely),

This misinterpreted line,

Yeah – "We shall overcome, indefinitely,

If we stand up and do something in time."

Dark

3/04/2018

Dark

I remember staring into the mirror,

And wondering why I was dark,

Why my skin wasn't like princesses',

Why it resembled a woody bark,

Cinderella was not black,

Let's not talk about Snow White,

Nah not even Ariel,

Then why was I as dark as the night,

This bothered me,

More than broken toys,

Or lost Barbie dolls,

Practically disrupted all my joys,

All my dolls looked so pretty,

They were fair and fairer than the word,

It was taught that white is beauty,

And dark or brown isn't pretty, it's turd,

So throughout childhood,

I only dreamt of, one day,

Being pretty,

Or being fair so to say,

Looking into the mirror,

I would touch my skin,

Just stare into the deep dark brown,

Trying to assuage my sin,

My self- esteem,

And my basic,

Understanding of beauty,

Was so wrong, so pathetic,

And as I grew up,

I realized that I wasn't alone,

There was something called "Racism",

Thousands of brown skinned people loathed their skin tone,

Who is to blame,

For this foolish bigotry,

Family? School? Society?

Or is it all three?

All the aunts and grand moms,

Constantly drill us to stay clean, clear and tidy,

Right from when we are barely four,

Because remember girls must be fair to pretty,

In school,

I always wondered why the illustrations,

Of all the textbooks,

Had fair skinned, perfect looking complexions,

Only fair and pretty girls,

Can be popular and perfect,

The first rule of teens right?

That's what we learn to accept,

And this is only because,

Humans have divided society,

Have shunned and labelled brown skin as dirty,

Forced the belief that only white is true beauty,

So stop telling your children,

That beauty,

Is fair and supple skin,

This should be a parental duty,

Stop advertising fairness creams,

Ointments and lotions,

Because neither do they work,

Nor do they spread the right notion,

Empower the dark skinned to believe,

That they are beautiful too,

That brown isn't turd,

It's like the soft, wet sand guarding the ocean blue,

Like silky brown chocolate,

Like the rough hard barks of chestnut trees,

Colouring the ground of mother earth,

Like the pale, fallen leaves carried by the autumn breeze,

Brown is beauty too,

Like the plush brown leather couch,

Or the rucky brown covering of a perfectly ripe coconut,

Or like a freshly ground coffee powder pouch,

Let us rewrite fairy tales,

Those princesses needn't be as white as snow,

Nor fairer than the word,

Instead let their characters steal the show,

So to all the kids,

Who stare at their brown flesh,

Every day, hoping to change it,

Don't trap yourself in that mesh,

Carry that darkish garb,

With pride,

You are beautiful, you are perfect,

Learn to love yourself and march on with a stride,

Humans need to change their perception,

Of 'white' and 'black' skin,

Because truthfully speaking,

The darkness only lies within.

2077

2077

After 75 years of life,

As I sit on my old green sofa,

With a fresh cup of tea,

Wearing an old, tweed sweater, knitted by my late mother,

Staring out of the window,

I look at all the concrete and brick, but all I see is a field of green and butterflies.

The flying cars sweep past me, but all I see is a flock of birds getting the best of the September breeze.

The dirty grey smog stares back, but all I see is a beautiful blue, a sky blue.

My granddaughter comes trotting in,

Loaded with VR gear and her robot, but all I see is a cup-saucer set and a Barbie doll.

Meanwhile, she orders the window to open and abracadabra! Yet all I see is a hard wooden frame with frosted glass and rusted grills, creaking at every push.

As the window opens, the humid, foul, polluted air comes in, yet all I smell is the damp soil of the August monsoons.

My grandson is in his room attending online school, but

all I see is a book covered with orange and a wooden desk.

The robo-cook gets us some amino bars, but all I see are fresh, almond cookies baked by my grandmother.

The lights run on solar and never ever even blink, but all I see is a wax candle burning,

Burning a warm orange, in the pitch black powercut night.

As I stare out of the window, I look at the world as it is, in reality, in the way it has changed over the last 75 years, the way it is now,

Yet,

All I see are my memories,

My youth,

My days,

My life.

Don't

10/11/2018

Don't

Don't question the pain inside you,

Don't ask where it comes from,

Don't let it overcome you,

Don't break the norm,

Don't let the tear slide down,

Don't tear your cheek with your nail,

Don't look in a mirror and sob,

Don't let your false smile fail,

Don't show you're hurt,

Don't ask for aid,

Don't sit alone in the bathroom stall,

Don't let your strength fade,

Don't yell out in agony,

Don't cry out your heart,

Don't bottle it up though,

Don't let it become your part,

Don't ever show your emotion,

Don't ever let them know,

Don't show them you're weak,

Because they'll just take advantage of your sorrow.

Bahadur

12/09/2019

Bahadur

The sky was wailing,

Wailing, just like the mother,

Dirty grey and dark clouds covered the sky,

As though Nature herself had lost a brother,

The boy was merely seventeen,

Living in the jungle,

Loved by his village and tribe,

Raised by his mother and his uncle,

As valiant as his late father-

Bahadur Singh,

This boy was always looking for an adventure,

He wanted to be the king,

He would go to the deep dark forests,

Stay for a week in there,

Capturing the wildest and challenging the finest creatures,

He wanted to enter the lion's lair,

So he took his axe,

Took his ring,

And without any delay he took off,

Towards the forest cutting,

He didn't hesitate,

Just walked right in,

Holding the axe,

He began mocking,

Mocking and challenging the lion,

He steadied his hand,

His prowess was such,

It made boars and bears look unmanned,

The lion took it all in,

And gave a nasty roar,

As though accepting the challenge,

He moved forward with a determined core,

The contestants eyed each other,

Calculating every move,

Slowly they advanced forward,

The boy attacked first with a terrible groove,

The lion dodged the threat,

But quickly came back,

Dug one claw into his hand,

Then tore the skin from off his back,

The power and force,

The strength of the notorious lion,

Was too much for a child of 17,

But the boy said he would rather die tryin',

The boy would lose,

It was for sure,

The lion was too powerful,

He could never endure,

The pain, the cuts,

All covered in blood,

The boy tried running,

But skid in the mud,

The lion roared once more,

A dark, evil and ravenous roar,

With a final stroke it cut the body,

Pushed its claw right into his core,

The boy just lay there, dead and gone,

Soon his body was found,

Half eaten, half rotten,

It became the talk of the town,

How one boy,

Had tried to avenge his father's death,

For this very lion had killed Bahadur,

And the boy had taken an oath on his funeral wreath,

To fulfill his father's dream,

By killing the lion,

Becoming the king,

He wasn't afraid of dying,

So he gave up his life,

Just like his father,

To achieve a baseless ambition,

And left alone his mother,

She stood horrified, staring at the body,

First her husband, now her son,

She couldn't understand their wish,

To be king or be none,

One thing was for sure,

There could be only one king,

The lion of the jungle,

It had proved its mettle by the killing,

The entire village was mourning,

They had lost two of their greatest,

Gathered in a little brick hut,

Remembering their brave adventures in the forest,

Bahadur had died on a similar day,

The storm was harsh,

Winds were uprooting trees and homes,

The streets were just marsh,

The sky was wailing,

Wailing just like the mother,

Dirty grey and dark clouds covered the sky,

As though Nature herself had lost a brother.

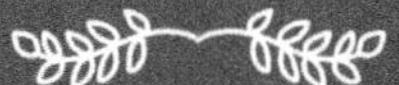

A colourful monochrome

29/08/18

A colourful monochrome

White,

Just the plain white ceiling of the hospital,

The first thing I saw after I opened my eyes,

The blanket around me, still white,

The coat of the doctor and the coat of the nurse,

White, welcoming white,

Over the next twelve months, Pink,

My room, my clothes, my toys,

Everything anyone ever gifted me,

Pink, baby pink,

Then the days began to change, blue,

Like the sky above which met the sea often,

The sky which I sat for hours gazing,

Diamond studded at night blue,

Like the water of the pool I jumped in,

Blue, sky blue,

My first day of school and yellow,

My bus, my shirt, my chair, my pencil,

The sun shining bright above,

Yellow, a warm yellow,

As I enter middle school, purple,

The jealousy, the fights,

The obsession of dressing up,

Cycling back home crying, under a purple thundering sky,

Purple, deep purple,

The first date, red dress, red lip,

The colour of my cheeks,

The wedding saree, draped like a queen,

Like Cupid blushing red,

Crimson Red,

A baby puking everywhere and green,

Celebrating adulthood by gardening green, like the fresh basil leaves,

The grass in the park where my son plays,

Like my smoothie to lose weight,

Green, fresh green,

The kid grows up and orange,

The labels on my son's boxes as he moves out,

The warm colour of sunset as I sit alone on the beach,

Like the tassel on his graduation cap,

And funny, the mask I apply to stop wrinkles,

Orange, bittersweet orange,

I'm feeling old now and grey,

The weakness, my pale skin and the platinum colour of my frail hair, grey,

The desolate hospital room staring back at me,

Like the rainy sky outside the window,

Grey, a tired grey,

I take my last breath and black,

Like the tenebrosity of the night,

The colour of my son's shirt at my funeral,

Like the doorway to death,

Black, pitch black.

Strength

18/04/2019

Strength

Like the jarring sound of an alarm,

The reports were thrown at me,

The doctor's countenance was glum,

I suddenly felt caged, no more free,

Tears rolled down my cheek,

My hands trembled and refused to move,

I sat alone, a mess, a wreck,

My heart's beat no longer a steady groove,

Life, they say, is short,

Well I didn't think it would be this way,

I was healthy, I was happy,

Now I'm scared I'll have to start counting day by day,

It takes a while,

A month or two, I don't keep track,

But soon I accept this challenge, I say,

Throw me to the wolves and I'll come out leading the pack,

I'm hurting on the inside,

But I've learned to be strong,

I'm ready to fight for my life,

I'm going to prove those reports wrong,

My family, my friends,

They've told me I'll be okay,

They are scared too, but they,

Refuse to leave my side, not tomorrow nor today,

They hold my hand in theirs,

And look me in the eye,

"You can do this my darling,

All you have to do is try,"

So I try, I fight, I cry, I smile,

Because to overcome your demons,

You have to face them,

My lost life, I'm now redeeming,

Like the hands of the clock,

Constantly ticking all day,

Moving forward obstinately,

That's how strong I'm gonna be, that's how strong I'm gonna stay.

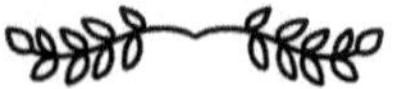

Move On

18/02/2019

Move On

You weren't there,
You never were,
I honestly see you everywhere,
It hurts that you still wanted her,

It meant nothing to your insensitive heart,
You never actually cared,
And my heart broke as you thrust in that dart,
The dart filled with the poison of your words,

My naïve soul's still searching your face,
Praying that this is just a nightmare,
Praying to wake up in a sober haze,
I'm slowly moving on, I swear,

It's funny to think that all this,
All that we had,
Was just momentary bliss,
I can't believe I'm so very sad,

Sad, and oh I care,

I still care after all that you put me through,

That's one of the many things we don't share,

Like how I was always true to you,

You promised me the world,

We made big plans,

And then you snatched everything away,

You crushed my heart with your bare hands,

But I'm done moping around,

I've taken enough,

I didn't deserve any of this,

So you better leave with all of your perfidious stuff,

And as you've moved onto your path,

I hope it never again crosses mine,

Cause we are done,

And that's how it's going to be till the end of time.

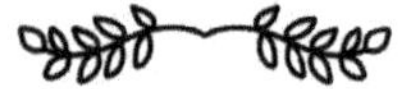

Hurt

03/11/2018

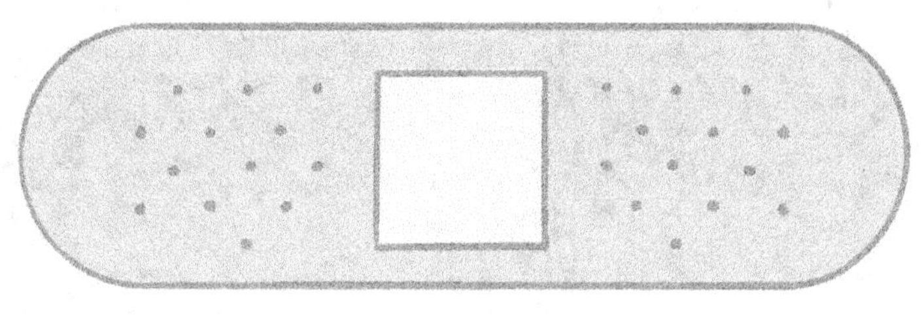

Hurt

I'm not giving up,

Not today,

They can't get me down,

No matter what they say,

It's not easy, no,

I feel it rising in my throat,

That fear, the doubt, the lonesome feeling,

I'm struggling to stay afloat,

I may be alone,

I may be unsure,

But I have myself, and

The power to cross through to shore,

No one cares,

They've made it pretty clear,

I don't need them,

I try to cover up the wound made by that shear,

It hurts you know,

It claws on my inside,

Burning my conscience,

Pushing me to hide,

I want to do so much,

Want to see this world,

Want this world to see me,

But I keep feeling pushed aside, blatantly hurled,

Does no one remember me,

Everything washed clean outta their mind,

I did all I could for them to like me,

I was even ready to step behind,

It's not about what I deserve anymore, no

It's much worse,

Because I'm not even getting what I don't deserve, and

The wound's becoming too deep to nurse,

The longer I keep ignoring what's truly bothering me,

The deeper that wound gets,

But it's like I'm immune to the pain,

It's like the fake smile my face invariably sets,

The people who are the most in pain,

Are the ones who always try to make others smile,

They don't realise it's in vain,

All of this, all generosity is so futile,

In the end the same people,

You gave everything to,

Are the ones who, directly or indirectly,

Turn their backs on you,

And then it's like a shard of glass,

Thrust right into my chest,

Except this one can't be pulled out like a knife,

This is the one which won't let me rest,

But my naïve heart still looks for good,

Accepting what's given,

And without thinking of my own pitiful state,

Every sinner is forgiven,

I promise myself I'll be more careful,

The next time,

But it never holds cause of my gullibility,

It's as though it is sublime,

And as the days go by I ask myself,

Is it worth it?

Why am I always in this mess?

Why only me, dammit?

But then I grow,

I mature and learn,

I am stronger now,

Not just another girl,

I've overcome my fears,

I don't care about the past,

I know they don't care,

And I don't even try to make it last,

It might sound crazy,

They'll say I'm insane,

I won't let that faze me,

Won't switch my lane,

They will yell, let them,

Abuse till their roofs are sore,

I don't hear a word anymore,

Cause me, I roar,

I'm picking up those broken bits,

Fixing myself up,

And suddenly they don't bother me at all,

Something's made them stop,

It takes some time,

I give it a thought or two,

And that's when I realise,

The reason for this behaviour, completely new,

The only time people can hurt you,

Is the time period between,

The day you were born and the day you realise why.

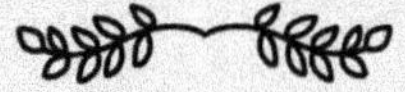

Treasure

18/08/2019

Treasure

I lay there on the hospital bed,
Cold, weak and tired,
Today was going to be my last,
I could feel it in every breath I respired,

My grandson sat by my bed,
Fiddling with his phone,
He was too young to recognise,
That I was dying and soon he'd be all alone,

I lost my son to the war,
His wife to grief,
Their little blue eyed boy,
Came to me, orphaned, crying in disbelief,

He was just 8 then,
Look how time passes by,
It's been 10 years from that day,
I look at him and let out a sigh,

"How do you feel now Grandpa?"
He asks with a concerned voice,
"I'm much better now my boy,"
I lie because I don't have a choice,

I beckon him towards me,
He comes and sits up straight,
"I want to tell you something,
My boy, and it just can't wait,"

"You're a man now, son,
You've got a life ahead of you,
I'm going to leave soon,
And then it'll be all down to you,"

I pause, look at him and then proceed,
"Life, son, is a haphazard series of events,
A mishmash of absurdities,
And of course you've gotta pay your rents,"

He chuckles at my last line,
I see the sparkle in his eye,
"It's scary how fast time goes by,
So make the most of it, well at least try,"

"Don't waste it all on chasing after money,
Don't waste it trying to get to the top,
Don't waste it staring at a screen,
Don't forget all the things you have to do before that heartbeat
stops,"

"Son, don't forget to look at the smaller things,
The details of this beautiful world, this beautiful life,
Like how the withered leaves rustle with the familiar wind,
Like the intricate, hexagonal bee hive,"

I steady my trembling hand,
As I lift it up to point to the outside sky,
"Don't forget luxuriant Mother Nature,
Skip NYC for a day and run into the fields of barley and rye,"

"Lay down on the terraces one night,
Staring at the captivating starry blue above,
Feel the rain soak you up in the thunder-y mid June showers,
Trust me all this will make you fall in love,"

"Sweet boy, the magic that this world embodies,
Can't be explained in mere words and phrase,
It has to be experienced,
And once you have, the memories you can't possibly erase,"

He leans forward,

I can see his gaze deepen,

I've got so much more to tell him,

But I feel tired now and soon I'll be sleeping,

My voice is now just a whisper,

In slow, broken, breathy words I continue,

"I want you to spend every minute of this god-given gift,

Living to the fullest, making all your dreams come true,"

"Do whatever you want, son,

So that when you lay here like me,

You don't have any regrets at all,

Death won't be a drudge, it'll simply set you free,"

My breath stung my nasal tract,

A tear slid down my face,

"You will always be my greatest treasure, son,"

The lights grew dim, now barely a feeble haze,

I felt his warm hand on mine,

I felt his head on my chest,

"And you'll always be my hero," he quietly said,

Then holding onto my treasure, I fell into perpetual rest.

Acknowledgement

This was my first book and there are some very important people who have helped me carve this simple blotch of wet clay into my little chiselled masterpiece. First and foremost, I'd like to thank my family. Mumma, Dad and Om - Thank you for being my biggest critics and at the same time my strongest pillars of support who have always encouraged me to keep writing. Had it not been for your patience and eagerness to listen to my poems, I probably would've stopped writing a long time ago.

Special thanks to my friends who've read my poems and given me crucial feedback which has only bettered my writing.

I am very grateful to the team at SuperFast Author, which has been very supportive and has helped me realize my dream. A big thank you to Priyanka Pachpande, for bringing my imagination to life through her illustrations. I'd also like to extend my gratitude to the wonderful staff at Star Copiers, especially Ajit, for everything that they've done for me.

Lastly I'd like to thank you for reading my book. It really means a lot to me.

Sera Gandhi